Hemel Hempstead

in old picture postcards

by
Dennis F. Edwards

European Library – Zaltbommel/Netherlands

GB ISBN 90 288 5797 4 / CIP

INTRODUCTION

It was called Hamelamestead by the Saxons, but the Romans were here before them. The remains of their villas have been found in Gadebridge and at Boxmoor.

In the Domesday Book, Hemel Hempstead appears to have been a rather insignificant place when compared with the entries for Berkhamstead and King's Langley. However, by the year 1150 it had a sizeable church, and a few centuries later, St. Mary's was one of the finest churches in Hertfordshire, its spire rising 200 ft above the small township. But the importance of Hemel Hempstead really began in 1539, when Henry VIII granted a charter creating the town a Bailiwick and the right to hold a Thursday market, plus a fair on the Feast of Corpus Christi. Unusually, the town remained a Bailiwick until the granting of a charter making it a Borough on 13th July 1898.

By the 17th century the market served a large area of this part of the county, and the historian John Norden records that, at Hemel Hempstead, the market was 'plentifull of all things necessary for the people's relief'.

By the 18th century there was an increasing number of water-powered mills along the banks of the Gade and the Bulbourne (which meet at Two Waters). In 1795 the Grand Junction Canal Act was passed and the waterway was completed through Boxmoor in 1804. The common lands of both Boxmoor and Two Waters were ancient 'wastes' and as early as 1594, the principal land owners and families set up a trust to ensure that the land would always be open to the public for grazing. The boundaries of the Moor have altered over the centuries, parts being sold for the canal and later for the construction of the London and Birmingham Railway (opened in 1837).

At the dawn of the railway age, paper making and light engineering were important local industries. In 1809 John Dickinson, inventor of a number of methods of improved paper production, bought Apsley Mills and by 1823 was employing sixty people.

Another Apsley industry, established in the early 19th century, was that of Kent Brushes (founded in London by William Kent the previous century).

In Hemel Hempstead itself, the engineering works of Joseph Cranstone was set up in 1798. Later the family were responsible for the building of the town's first gas work. In 1867, the son of the founder, also named Joseph, constructed a steam road carriage. He drove this successfully to London. But disaster struck on the return, when the carriage was destroyed after getting out of control on Stanmore Hill. The firm in that time advertised its 'French velocipeds' which, the reader was assured, could easily achieve a speed of 8 or 12 miles per hour 'with a little practice'. Later the company became the Hemel Hempstead Engineering Company and were still in business after the Second World War.

But Hemel Hempstead was predominantly an agricultural town. In 1822, William Cobbett was uncharacteristically pleased when he reached the town: 'The wheat is good all the way. The barley and oats are good enough until I came to Hemel Hempstead. But the land along here is very fine, the land is, in short, excellent and it is real corn country.'

By the later decades of the 19th century Hemel Hempstead was a favoured place for residents, and some development of houses and villas began for London commuters. The prospective buyers of houses at Crouchfield were offered a free season ticket for a year on the London and North Western Railway. The Midland Railway reached Hemel Hempstead in 1877, with a line from Harpenden, and Alexandra Road, Broad Street and Midland Road were developed for commuter houses – the area being known as New Town. The Midland Line also reached the gas works near the Euston main line, but there was never any through-connecting train service, although a halt was opened at Heath Park in 1906. Passenger services were 'temporarily withdrawn' from the line in 1947, never to be reinstated. Goods traffic lingered on until about 1958.

John Dickinson's paper mills were by far the largest employer in the area, and there were 5,000 men and women on the payroll in the late 1930s. Many of these workers came from other places, and a station was opened on the LMS line in 1938 to improve travel connections. Yet at this time, one could soon be out of the industrial and residential areas and up on to the open hills. Hemel Hempstead was still a country town.

In 1946, news of great changes to come were announced in London. At a stormy meeting in Hemel Hempstead, Lewis Silkin (later Lord Silkin), the Minister of Town and Country Planning, told residents that the area had been designated as the site for one of the proposed London 'overspill' towns. On 4th February 1947, the Government purchased 5,910 acres of land around the area and work began on the New Town. By April 1949, the first of the new residents moved into their exciting new homes, leaving the drab streets of London for a fresh life on the hills above the town. Progress came ever more rapidly; the old farming hamlets became new suburbs. Parades of shops, schools and community centres sprang up on what had been rolling cornfields. Marlowes was redeveloped as the main shopping centre. Old Hemel Hempstead began to fade away. The High Street, which in the 1940's had branches of Woolworths and Montague Burton, found itself a ghost town, at least for a time.

But, despite all the changes (and to be fair, some of them have made great improvements to the local scene), much of historic interest survives. Old postcards of the Hemel Hempstead area have proved surprisingly difficult to find, but this collection will, one hopes, awake old memories, as well as a new interest for those who came to the area in recent times.

Ickenham, Uxbridge
January 1994
Dennis F. Edwards

1. An early multi-view card of Hemel Hempstead. The churches (top centre of the card) are St. Mary's (left) and St. Mary's, Apsley. Other pictures are of Gadebridge park, the canal and High Street.

2. The parish church of ancient Hemel Hempstead dates from 1140 and is one of the finest in Hertfordshire. It has a superb Norman west door. The 200 ft high spire was completed in the year 1340. The historian Chauncey wrote in 1700: 'A very fair and tall spire, covered with lead, which is a great ornament to the town.'

3. St. Mary's, Hemel Hempstead, from the Gade meadows. The south transept dates from the 15th century. The church was restored in Victorian days, and the spire in 1979-1983.

4. A view of the old town from Gadebridge Park in the 1920's. On the right stood The Bury, the estate of the Coombes family.

5. The Charter Tower, formerly the entrance to The Bury. The house was built by Sir Richard Coombes in 1595 on the site of an earlier mansion. The Elizabethan house had 14 rooms 'all finely furnished'. The building was demolished in the early 19th century.

6. The Thursday Market about 1906. The market was held here until it was removed to Marlowes in the 1950's. The gabled building on the left stands on the site of The Leg Inn (1671). The Bell Inn is on the far side of a narrow passageway called Old Plait Market (now Austin's Place). Here, finished straw plait was sold to the representatives of the hat manufacturers of Luton and other towns.

7. High Street and the Corn Exchange in 1905. The plaque on the side of the building (left) commemorates the granting of the charter to the small town of Hemel Hempstead by Henry VIII in 1539, creating it as a Bailiwick, with the right to hold a weekly market. The head of Henry VIII is at the top of the plaque.

8. High Street, with the Town Hall on the left. The street was originally known as Market Street. The shops on the left include Henry Stevens' 'Shoe Mart' and the historic Bell Inn.

9. The Town Hall, built in 1851. The ancient Bell Inn (left) was the most important of the town's hostelries. In 1750 it had nine beds and stabling for 54 horses. The Bell played an important part in the social life of the town and the Bailiff and members of the town vestry frequently met here for social events.

10. High Street 1902 with one of Joseph Cranstone's water pumps, surmounted by a gas lamp. Gas lighting was first introduced in High Street in September 1835. The Bailiff entertained forty guests at The Bell to celebrate. The first gas works were in Bury Road.

11. Despite the vast expansion of Hemel Hempstead in the last 125 years, the north end of High Street still ends abruptly with the country beyond. The Brewers Inn is on the left. The buildings on the right contain the Slaters, makers of baskets. The family owned High Street Farm nearby from the 16th century. The shop moved to Boxmoor about ten years ago.

12. High Street 1900. The Boot (right) was first mentioned in 1725. Also on the right is the London and County Bank.

13. Looking up High Street 1903. The second shop on the left is that of H.T. Hart, baker and confectioner. Many of the buildings in High Street date from the second half of the 18th century, following a disastrous fire in 1749.

14. Alexandra Road and adjacent streets were once known as the 'New Town', when they were laid out following the coming of the Midland Railway from Harpenden in 1877. The Congregational Church dates from 1890, the foundation stone being laid on 3rd June of that year. The building stands on the site of a temporary iron chapel, donated by local industrialist Joseph Cranstone in 1880.

15. The Broadway shops were considered a vast step forward in modern shopping in Edwardian days. In the distance can be seen the London and County Bank building.

16. The entrance gates to Gadebridge Park, with the old fire station on the right. The first fire brigade was founded in November 1845. By 1884 there were two manual fire engines, twelve paid firemen and twelve volunteers.

17. The fountain was presented to the town by the Misses Ann and Helen Varney to commemorate the creation of Hemel Hempstead as a Borough on 13th July 1898.

18. Gadebridge Park was the home of the Paston-Cooper family. In 1774 the estate was described as being in 'a pleasant and plentiful country not half a mile from the church and town of Hemel Hempstead, and 29 miles on a Turnpike road from London, to and from which a stage coach travels three times a week'.

19. Ornamental foot bridge and water splash over the Gade with the driveway leading up to the edge of the High Street.

20. A peaceful scene on the Gade in Gadebridge Park in 1906. The owner of the estate at this time was Sir Astley Paston-Cooper, first Mayor of the town in 1898.

21. Bury Hill looking towards Bury Mill and the old town in 1912. Frederick Griggs in his book on Hertfordshire, published about this time, tells us of the view from the Jolly Dragon looking eastwards from the town 'where the hills are covered over with corn'.

22. Hemel Hempstead in the First World War. Army camp at Gadebridge Park in July 1917. The writer of the card, Private Cripps, tells his mother in Maidstone (Kent) that he is sitting outside one of the huts recovering from an inoculation.

23. London and North Western Railway bus in Marlowes en route to Boxmoor Station in 1907. This bus service operated 21 times a day from the Posting House at 1, Marlowes. On the left are the Public Baths, opened in 1866.

24. The southern end of Marlowes – a scene that has been utterly swept away in the development of the mid-20th century. The first houses appeared in Marlowes towards the end of the 18th century and by Victorian days, the area was described as one of the most unhealthy in the area because of bad drainage. The street contained the Princess Theatre and the Luxor Cinema (the latter closed in August 1960).

25. The Baptist church in Marlowes, built in 1860.

26. How it all looked in 1920. The white house bottom left is the Heath Park Hotel, with Cotterells. Alongside are the sidings from the Midland Railway. The line itself curves away across what is now the site of Kodak House, to cross Marlowes by the Albion Mill at Moor End. The railway bridge was demolished at midnight on 6th July 1960 in preparation for the huge new road project that transformed this area of the town.

27. King's College Convalescent Home (Cheere House). The house was originally the home of Sir John Sebright. The adjacent West Herts Infirmary was opened in 1877 by the Duchess of Teck. In 1899 it was the first hospital in Britain to have X-ray equipment.

28. The original Hemel Hempstead Station stood above the old town on the Midland Railway branch line from Harpenden and was opened on 16th July 1877. Passenger trains were withdrawn 'as a temporary measure' in 1947, but never restored, but freight traffic survived until 1958. The steam locomotive used in the last years was affectionately known by local people as 'Puffing Annie'.

29. A curious railway experiment of 1931 – the LMS 'Ro-railer', a road bus that could also run along railways. It was an attempt to fight road competition. The 'Nicky Line', as the Hemel Hempstead branch was locally known, was used to demonstrate the vehicle to the press. The bus was built by Karrier Motors and is seen here at Harpenden ready to start for Hemel Hempstead. On the platform are Lord Stamp (Chairman of the LMS) and Sir Alfred Yarrow, engineer.

30. Moor End with The Plough public house and the war memorial (unveiled by Lt. Col. Smeathman in June 1921). The whole of this area is now occupied by the famous traffic roundabout (said to be one of the most complicated in Hertfordshire) and also Kodak House.

31. On the Grand Union Canal at Boxmoor by Station Road bridge. The Fellows Morton and Co. boat is towing a second craft, known as a 'butty boat'. Freight traffic on the canal came to an end by the close of the 1950's.

32. St. John's Church, Boxmoor, and Station Road in 1907. The building was designed by Paul Waterhouse in 1874 and enlarged in 1893.

33. The first church at Boxmoor was a Chapel of Ease in 1829. Boxmoor parish was formed in 1844. The first vicar, the Reverend A.C. Richards, built the vicarage in Heath Lane at his own expense.

34. Interior of St. John's Church about 1913. The east window is in memory of the Reverend Thomas White.

35. The canal looking west. In the distance are Foster Brothers saw mills (closed in 1969). The cottages on the right were known as Moor or Star Cottages (there was a small pub of that name here). They were demolished in 1934 and the site was grassed over.

36. Boxmoor Lock. Beyond the trees on the right distance were Boxmoor's open-air baths. They were created in what had been pits, from which chalk had been dug in connection with the building of the canal at the start of the 19th century. There were two pools – one free and the other by subscription. They closed in 1934.

37. Pair of canal craft working through Boxmoor locks in 1933. The canal was still busy with traffic at this time and John Dickinson and Company exported paper from their mills every weekday to London. The 25 ft long craft left Apsley at 5 p.m. and arrived at Paddington Basin, in London at 7 a.m.

38. The Fishery Inn was always a popular stopping place for thirsty canal men. The road bridge seen here was built in 1922, replacing the original 19th century bridge.

39. Beyond The Fishery Inn were the watercress beds and the water meadows along the Bulbourne by the Chaulden House estate. This was the ornamental water tower with the falls in 1907.

40. The water tower and the river Bulbourne looking towards Old Fishery Lane. Watercress was a very important import product in the Hemel Hempstead area and something like 15% of all watercress grown in England came from here. The cress was sent to London in special baskets by train from Boxmoor station.

41. Boxmoor, looking towards the old Midland Railway and Heath Park Halt (opened in 1906). The building with the clock is Boxmoor Public Hall. It opened in 1889, financed by the Boxmoor Trust. The architect was W.A. Foster. Next door is the old Heath Park Hotel, which in 1869 advertised: 'Fitted with every appliance for the comfort and convenience of gentlemen and travellers.'

42. The Moor looking west. The distant row of cottages includes the Steam Carriage public house, named after Joseph Cranstone's partly successful road steam carriage experiment of 1867.

43. Looking towards the Crouchfield area of Boxmoor, in about 1912.

44. St. John's Road, with the Roman Catholic church of St. Mary and St. Joseph, which was built in 1898. The Three Blackbirds public house dates from at least 1760.

45. St. John's Road about 1902. The shop on the right is Hollicks, newsagent and hairdresser's.

46. Fishery Road near the junction with Horsecroft Road. The first residents of these houses were given free season tickets for a year to London.

47. Hammerfield (spelt 'Hammesfield' on this card of 1907) was an early attempt to build low-cost housing and small industrial units in the 1880's. It was not a success and the area became known as 'the deserted village'.

48. Hammerfield was also called 'Little Switzerland' because of the fir trees planted here by the developers. This is a view down Glenview Road in 1908.

49. Old Hemel Hempstead included many small settlements. This is Green End. The larger houses were Green End House and Belgrave House. The later was the home of Paul Waterhouse, architect of St. John's Church.

50. Lockers Park. The estate was called 'Lockyeras' in 1491 and in the 17th century 'Lookers'. In 1677, the estate was owned by Francis King, Bailiff of Hemel Hempstead.

51. London Road and the Swan Inn at the junction of Box Lane. The small building next door is the lodge to Boxmoor House, once the estate of the Blackwood family. At one time the house was a home for 'the imbicile children of gentlefolk'. It was also a hospital in the First World War.

52. London Road looking towards the original LNWR oblique bridge of 1837. The bridge was constructed by the famous firm of William and Louis Cubitt (contractors for the new railway, from King's Langley to Tring). 'All men of science' were urged to visit what was then a unique bridge.

53. Boxmoor and the Bulbourne. The tower of the Baptist Church of 1825 and the houses of Russell Street and Catherine Street can be seen. This area of Boxmoor was known as Duck Hall.

54. General view of the Crouchfield area of Boxmoor from Roughdown in the 1900's. Boxmoor station is in the foreground. Over to the left, above the station, is the Fishery Inn, and in the distance are the grounds of Green End House.

55. View from Roughdown of the Two Waters area. The Baptist Church and Brockman Hall and the houses of Russell Place can be seen. When the canal was being constructed in the early 19th century, the 'navvies' had a camp here in Roughdown.

56. The Railway Hotel and the approach to Boxmoor Station. The station master's house is just visible to the right.

57. In 1906 villas, bungalows and houses were being advertised on ‘well drained, healthy sites at Boxmoor abuting the Common’ and prospective purchasers were assured that a ‘frequent and rapid service of Railway Company buses connects the estate with Hemel Hempstead’.

58. Chalk pit at Roughdown Common. The extraction of chalk was an important industry here until about 1912. The tunnels under the Common became unsafe because of the vibration from the nearby railway and they were sealed in 1916.

59. Sheethanger Common with the golf course, said to be one of the oldest in England. The Common was purchased by the Boxmoor Trust for £100 in 1886.

60. Felden Lane has little changed since this photograph was taken in 1908. Felden, one of the ancient hamlets around Hemel Hempstead, means 'field end', or a settlement of the edge of the cultivated land.

61. Felden Lodge, for many years the National Training Centre for the Boys' Brigade.

62. The Grand Union Canal near Bourne End in 1906. Commercial traffic on the canal had reached its peak about this time. The period after the Second World War saw an ever declining trade and the last regular use by commercial craft was in the late 1950's. But the canal today is a popular route for holiday boats.

63. Water cress growing was an important industry at Two Waters. To the left is The Bell Inn, a changing place for the coach to Leighton Buzzard in pre-railway days. On the very far right can be seen the gas holder of the Boxmoor, Two Waters and Crouchfield Gas Light and Coke Company, founded in 1868 and later served by the old Midland branch line.

64. Apsley Lock, with Durrants Hill in the distance. The canal ran alongside Dickinson's paper mills and the company used the canal for exporting its products for many years, with daily boats leaving for London.

65. The spire of St. Mary's Church, Apsley. The church was dedicated in 1871 and became a separate parish from Hemel Hempstead in May 1875. The cost of the building was mostly bourne by Charles Longman and the directors of John Dickinson.

66. The London Road at Apsley with John Dickinson's staff leaving the premises on an afternoon in 1934. A station was opened on the nearby LMS line on 22nd September 1938 by Lord Stamp, Chairman of the LMS, and Sir Reginald Buner, Chairman of John Dickinson, the 13.00 p.m. stopping train from Euston breaking a special tape spread across the slow lines.

67. The charms of water meadows, picturesque old mills and the canal in the 1920's brought excursionists by both rail and bus. This is a poster produced by the London General Omnibus Company in 1921.

68. Leverstock Green is now part of the new development of Hemel Hempstead. The hamlet was originally a centre of the brick-producing trade. The church was built in 1849 (a separate parish from Hemel Hempstead was formed in 1850).

69. Water End is another hamlet on the river Gade and has been untouched by the expansion of modern Hemel Hempstead. This is the girls' school in about 1902.

70. One of the important country houses in the area is Gaddesden Place, for many years the home of the Halsey family. The house was built by James Wyatt in 1774, but largely reconstructed after a disastrous fire in 1906.

71. A romantic view of the Hemel Hempstead countryside in Edwardian days. Cottages like this were a feature of many of the old hamlets in the area. But they were insanitary places. Whilst the men worked on the land, the women of the family would be engaged in the straw plaiting trade.

72. In the upper part of the Gade valley is the small village of Little Gaddesden, with the memorial to local men who fell in the First World War.

73. The first residents of Hemel Hempstead New Town arrived in 1949. This is a view of Queen's Square, Adeyfield, about 1961.

74. The new Hemel Hempstead. The mills and factories and rows of working class houses have been swept away from the back of Marlowes and the banks of the Gade have been transformed into pleasure gardens. This photograph dates from the early 1970's.

75. Hemel Hempstead in 1910. The Midland Railway runs across the foreground, with the haystacks of Handpost Farm. To the right is the Sunday School building next to St. Paul's Church in Queen Street.

76. Hemel Hempstead old and new: a multi-view card of 1960 with scenes that include Apsley, Boxmoor and the canal and High Street, as well as Adeyfield.